Other Books by Dr. Alveda King

IMAGES
THE ARAB HEART
WHO WE ARE IN CHRIST JESUS
I DON'T WANT YOUR MAN, I WANT MY OWN
SONS OF THUNDER: THE KING FAMILY LEGACY

Music Projects

LATTER RAIN - DVD
LET FREEDOM RING - CD

How Can the Dream Survive If We Murder the Children?

ABORTION IS NOT A CIVIL RIGHT!

By Dr. Alveda C. King

www.kingforamerica.com
www.priestsforlife.org/africanamerican
With Foreword by Father Frank Pavone
Edited by Brian Young

"...We have to look much deeper than that if we are to find the real cause of man's problems and the real cause of the world's ills today. ...Look in the hearts and souls of men.

...When you discover what you will be in your life, set out to do it as if God Almighty called you to do it. ...Do such a good job that the living, the dead or the unborn couldn't do it any better."

- Dr. Martin Luther King, Jr.

authorHOUSE®

AuthorHouse™
1663 Liberty Drive, Suite 200
Bloomington, IN 47403
www.authorhouse.com
Phone: 1-800-839-8640

First published by AuthorHouse   2/5/2008

ISBN: 978-1-4343-6150-9 (sc)

Printed in the United States of America
Bloomington, Indiana

This book is printed on acid-free paper.

Dedication

All honor, glory and praise to
Father God, Son Lord Jesus and Holy Spirit!

For my children
Jarrett and Family
Eddie (You asked me to write this book Thank you!)
Celeste
Jennifer
Joshua
John
Raphael
Phillip
Jessica
Mother Naomi
My Entire Family
Believers' Bible Christian Church
My Friends, Donors, and Supporters
including but not limited to:
Priests for Life
Silent No More Awareness Campaign
Rachael's Vineyard
National Pro-Life Radio
National Black Pro-Life Union
Operation Outcry
LEARN
Georgia Right to Life
Heartbeat International

For Generations to Come!

Table of Contents

 **Foreword**

Jesus defined his ministry with these words from the prophet Isaiah: "The spirit of the Lord is upon me. He has anointed me to proclaim liberty to the captive, to let the oppressed go free." This is the mission of the Church, and therefore of each Christian individual and Christian movement. It is the mission of the civil rights movement and it is the mission of the pro-life movement.

For years in my own pro-life work, I have been quoting Dr. Martin Luther King, Jr., in his affirmation of the sanctity of human life. He and his brother, Rev. A. D. King (Alveda's father) did not simply fight for the equality of the black person. They fought for the equality of everyone. Eliminating segregation was a corollary of a more fundamental imperative, namely, eliminating all oppression against human life.

When I met Alveda, she was already speaking out at pro-life events on a part time basis. I began to invite her to partner with our ministry more extensively. In his famous speech, "I Have a Dream," Dr. King spoke of Protestants and Catholics working together. The pro-life movement has become one of the most fruitful arenas for interdenominational collaboration, and Alveda's partnership with Priests for Life is yet another instance of it. One of Alveda's friends once shared with her the observation that our ministry together represents a union of the priestly and prophetic anointing that is stirring in many ways among the People of God.

The first time Alveda and I walked side by side in the annual March for Life in Washington, DC, on January 22, I asked her, "Does this remind you of the civil rights movement and the marches with your dad and uncle?" She responded, "Fr. Frank, this is the civil rights movement!"

This book is a heartfelt proclamation of that truth.

For years, I've sat in pro-life strategy meetings in which leaders have asked, "How do we get African Americans more involved in the pro-life movement? That question, however, is not properly phrased. The question really is, "How do we assist our African American brothers and sisters to understand that the pro-life movement belongs just as much to them as it belongs to anyone else?" Our black brothers and sisters should not feel like they have to join a white movement in order to defend life; nor need they join a Republican movement or any other kind of movement. They simply need to be themselves: to bring their passion for justice to bear on the unborn children, to bring their vigor for fighting violence and inequality to the fight against abortion, to raise their voices on the streets of America again, this time on behalf of children in the womb!

In the process of doing so, it is not necessary to abandon any of the other concerns they voice or issues they embrace. It is simply to allow the dream if Dr. King to embrace every segment of the human family, and to sing once more – this time in the name of the unborn – "We Shall Overcome!"

Father Frank Pavone
National Director, Priests for Life
President, National Pro-Life Religious Council

 **Introduction**

Dear readers,

In 1983, my life took a dramatic turn. I accepted Jesus Christ as my Lord and Savior.

Now, I know just what you're thinking. Wasn't I born into the famous King family, headed by preachers on every side? Why would it take a "church girl" like me to advance well into adulthood to become a Christian?

Well, I did, in fact, grow up in the pews, but I didn't know Jesus for real in my youth. I didn't know Jesus personally.

When I accepted Jesus Christ as Lord, my life changed forever. I repented for many acts and deeds, including my two abortions. To repent is to change and be changed. This book is a collection of expressions, experiences and lessons learned since my second birth.

My son Eddie, who was rescued from the abortionist's knife by his great grandfather Daddy King and by his dad, both strong black men who refused to help me make another big mistake, has been asking me to write this book for years. If I had acted upon every suggestion Eddie has made over the years, I would be light years ahead!

You'll find that in this book I quote particular statements made by my uncle, Dr. Martin Luther King, Jr., several times. My uncle knew that the principle of restatement, saying something over and over, helps to get a point across. I now use this principle as well to get a point across; make no mistake about it. Dr. King was pro-life!

While I have made many speeches, written several articles, contributed to other authors, this is my first book on the subject of abortion. There are many warriors who have fought harder for the unborn, who have been in the trenches longer, and who deserve your attention. Please seek them out. It is my prayer that this book will inspire you to choose life, to learn about the battle for the voiceless and helpless, and to join the ranks of the faithful as we march on in victory.

God bless you!

><> Alveda

1.
How Can The Dream Survive If We Murder The Children?

My uncle, Dr. Martin Luther King, Jr. once stirred the soul of our nation with a speech on the steps of the Lincoln Memorial. The speech was at the end of another long summer in the long struggle for equal justice. He spoke that day of a Dream, "a dream that one day this nation will rise up and live out the true meaning of its creed; we hold these truths to be self-evident, that all men are created equal."

Drawing from the Old Testament Book of Amos, he declared, "… [W]e will not be satisfied until justice rolls down like waters and righteousness like a mighty stream."

My Uncle Martin had a Dream. It is my Dream today.

For today, there is an entire class of Americans who face discrimination under the law, who are treated like property, and who are regarded by some as sub-human. They are held by our courts as unworthy of legal protection, just as the courts once held slaves. They are innocent of any wrongdoing, yet persecuted because of who they are.

1

My Dream, shared by millions, is that our nation will rise up and correct these great injustices – injustices against those living in the womb.

* *

A woman, as any person, has rights. Because of those rights, she can choose what she does with her body in almost every instance. Her baby, though, is not her body. A woman and her baby are two distinct human beings, each endowed by their Creator with the right to life, a personal right that cannot be matched, much less trumped, by any other.

Let me be clear. In the debate over abortion, the foremost civil right is the child's. Our Declaration of Independence states that we are endowed by our Creator with certain inalienable rights and that among these are life, liberty, and the pursuit of happiness. Life is listed first because it's the most fundamental right. This is truly self-evident: without life, no other rights exist.

And so I ask, how can the Dream survive if we murder the children? If we are to live out the true meaning of our nation's creed, how can we treat some people like they're not people?

Every baby scheduled for abortion is like a slave in the womb of his or her mother. The mother decides his or her fate and does so at will. In the ongoing travesty of the debate over whether abortion and infanticide should be condoned, a voice in the wilderness continues to cry out, "What about the children?"

We have been fueled by the fire of "women's rights" for decades. The talk from those who think that taking the life of an unborn human being is a right focuses on women, but not all women. We have heard pro-abortion talk for so long that we have become deaf to the outcry of the real victims whose rights are being trampled upon, the babies and the mothers who once carried them.

We don't hear from abortion advocates about a mother's right to know the serious consequences and repercussions of making a decision to abort her child. More pointedly, we don't hear about the rights of the women who have been called to pioneer the new frontiers of the new millennium only to have their lives snuffed out before the calendar even turns.

Oh God, what would Martin Luther King, Jr., who dreamed of having his children judged by the content of their characters, do if he'd lived to see the contents of untold numbers of children's skulls emptied into the bottomless caverns of the abortionists' pits?

What terribly mixed signals we send to our society today; they reflect our moral confusion. We allow and even encourage our young to engage in promiscuous sex. When their sin conceives, we pretty much tell them, "Your babies aren't really babies if you don't want them to be -- let our abortion facilities erase them from your lives."

We march to cure breast cancer, yet promote an unnatural, violent procedure that has become one of its contributors. We say birth control is the answer to unwanted pregnancy, yet abortion advocates themselves tell us that half the women who abort were using birth control when they conceived.

Simply stated, we are suffering a disconnection from logic and reality, a disconnection driven by our sinful wills. I know. Believe me, I know.

I am a mother of six living children and I am a grandmother. I am also a post-abortive mother. In the early 1970s, I suffered one involuntary and one voluntary abortion.

It happened like this. My uncle, Dr. Martin Luther King, Jr., was killed in 1968. I was married the next year. My father, Rev. A. D. King, Dr. King's brother, walked me down the aisle. Dad was also a civil rights leader, a primary strategist working with his brother. During the "Movement," Dad's house and church had been bombed. He had been jailed and experienced several threats against his life.

One week after the wedding, Dad was found dead in our home swimming pool, with no water in his lungs, and a bruise on his head. Needless to say, our family was in shock once again. In the midst of our grief, our family received the news that a new life was present. Alveda was pregnant! So, in the midst of our tears, we were able to smile at the hope of a new life.

A son was born and everyone welcomed him. Then, the tide turned again. My involuntary abortion was performed just prior to *Roe v. Wade* by my private physician without my consent.

I had gone to the doctor to ask why my cycle had not resumed after the birth of my son. I did not ask for and did not want an abortion. The doctor said, "You don't need to be pregnant, let's see." He proceeded to perform a painful examination which resulted in a gush of blood and tissue emanating from my womb. He explained that he had performed a "local D and C." Having no understanding of medical procedures, I didn't realize that my baby was dead.

Of course, lack of knowledge did not prevent me from experiencing the affects of post-abortion trauma. My body was sore, I began to develop breast inflammation, depression, and weight problems. I was argumentative, and my young husband didn't know what to do. We argued a lot and finally divorced.

In 1973, we tried to reconcile. It was shortly after the *Roe v. Wade* decision. During this season, I became pregnant again. There was adverse pressure and the threat of violence from the baby's father, my ex-husband. Because I was away from my family and church base, I caved in.

I became a client of Planned Parenthood. I went to the doctor and was advised that I didn't have to have the baby, which wasn't a baby yet anyway. At that office, they called him a blob of tissue. They said the procedure would hurt no more than "having a tooth removed." I made the fateful and fatal decision to abort our child.

The next day, I was admitted to the hospital. My medical insurance paid for the abortion. As soon as I woke up, I knew that something was very wrong. I felt very ill and very empty. I tried to talk to the doctor and nurses about it. They assured me that "it will all go away in a few days. You will be fine." They lied.

It did hurt, it didn't go away, and I wasn't fine.

Over the ensuing years, I experienced medical problems. I had trouble bonding with my son and his five siblings who were born after the abortions. I again began to suffer from eating disorders and depression, but now there were also nightmares, sexual dysfunctions, and a host of other issues. I felt angry about both abortions, but very guilty about the abortion I chose to have. The guilt made me very ill. I went through cervical surgery as a result of the abortions and had problems with my mammary system as well.

The aftermath was ongoing. My birthday is January 22, and each year this day is marred by the fact that it is the anniversary of Roe v. Wade, the harbinger of death to over 40 million babies. I, my two aborted children, and, I believe, my miscarried child are all direct victims of abortion. But abortion also has indirect victims. *Roe v. Wade* has adversely affected the lives of my entire family.

My children have all suffered from knowing that they had a brother or sister who their mother chose to abort. Often they ask if I ever thought about aborting them. Honestly, how could they not wonder? When they say, "You killed our baby," how could they not ache?

Abortion has been very painful for all of us. My mother and grandparents were very sad to know about the loss of the babies. In fact, it was my Grandfather, Daddy King, who helped keep me from aborting my fourth child, a son.

My grandfather, Dr. Martin Luther King, Sr., said no to abortion at least twice in my lifetime. The first time was when my mother Naomi was pregnant with me and considered an abortion. Mother's mom, Bessie had told my mother to ask Daddy to wear a "raincoat" (condom). Mother was clueless and she and Dad conceived me.

My birth would mark the end of Mother's dreams of college. Mama Bessie told Daddy King that my mother was thinking about abortion. He told Mother "No!" He had seen me in a dream three years before. I would be a bright skinned, red headed little girl who would bring great joy. His dream helped save my life! When I was born, my daddy named me Alveda Celeste King; Veda being a derivative of Vitae for life and Celeste to get me as close to Heaven as he could.

Years later, I was as far away from Heaven as I could be. Dating, which was a problem because of the related sexual sin, led me to pregnancy. Courting, from a position of abstinence or celibacy is good. Courting should lead to marriage without sex outside the marriage bed. But, I was dating. I asked the baby's daddy for the money for an abortion. He said, "No, it is murder. You are not going to kill a child of mine."

Thank God for my first baby's father and Daddy King!

Tragically, two of Daddy King's grandchildren had already been aborted without his knowledge when he saved the life of his next great-grandson. When I again became pregnant and considered abortion, he said, "No one is going to kill a grandchild of mine."

I don't want to leave the wrong impression about my story. Today, the aborted children's father also regrets the abortions. That any of us change our minds about abortion after the fact is not unexpected; even if we think we want an abortion at the time, we are almost always conflicted about it because we know at some level that it's wrong.

This is often the case at abortion mills. When couples come in, frequently the fathers don't want to kill the babies. Other times, the mothers don't want to abort, but feel pressured. What all of us, women and men, need at such a crucial time is someone to help us make the right decision for life!

I know that Someone.

I pray often for deliverance from the pain caused by my decision to abort. I thank God for the Christ centered healing ministry of Rachel's Vineyard where I received counseling. Truly, for me, and countless abortive mothers, nothing on earth can fully restore what has been lost. Only Jesus can. The only healing and redemption is in the blood of Jesus, blood willingly shed so that we could stand today and cry out for the blood of the unborn that is drenching the land of our children.

And so I speak, because I first decided to seek.

Today, my mother Naomi and I join the voices of thousands across America who are SILENT NO MORE. As part of the Silent No More Awareness Campaign, we can no longer sit idly by and allow this horrible spirit of murder cut down, yes cut out and cut away our unborn and destroy the lives of mothers. And make no mistake, once a woman becomes pregnant, she is forever a mother from that moment.

It is time for America, perhaps the most blessed nation on earth, to lead the world in repentance and restoration of life! If only we could carry the freedom of repentance to its fullest potential. If only America could repent and turn away from the sins of our nation.

I can only beseech the powers that be to hearken to the voice of the Lord and remember that human life is sacred. By taking the lives of our young, and wounding the wombs and lives of their mothers, we are flying in the face of God.

And God will not be mocked. If we continue down this path of destruction, we will be met at the gates by our own doom. If we refuse to answer the cry of mercy from the unborn, and ignore the suffering of the mothers, then we are signing our own death warrants.

My Uncle Martin stood for those who have been denied their rights. This non-violent servant of God was a staunch advocate of non-violence. He would never have condoned the mass destruction of innocent babies that has happened since Roe v. Wade. My Uncle Martin, who once said, "The Negro cannot win as long as he is willing to sacrifice the futures of his children for immediate personal comfort and safety," would have been appalled at what has happened to the aborted futures of so many babies.

Had he lived, I believe my Uncle Martin would be standing with me today. It was Martin who sounded the alarm against genocide in his Letter from a Birmingham Jail:

"Whenever the early Christians entered a town, the people in power became disturbed and immediately sought to convict the Christians for being "disturbers of the peace" and "outside agitators"' But the Christians pressed on, in the conviction that they were "a colony of heaven," called to obey God rather than man. Small in number, they were big in commitment. They were too God intoxicated to be "astronomically intimidated." By their effort and example they brought an end to such ancient evils as infanticide and gladiatorial contests."

Generally, we are more familiar with Dr. King's "I Have A Dream" speech. We focus on the words in that message, and often forget that the dream includes everyone, including the little ones in the womb.

I, like my Uncle Martin, have a dream. It's in my genes! I have a dream that all of us, the men and women, the boys and girls of America, will come to our senses and humble ourselves before God Almighty; that we will pray for mercy and receive His healing grace. I have a dream that our nation will finally rise up and truly live our creed that all men are created equal. Every human being is entitled to life, liberty, justice and the pursuit of happiness. There must be no other way. This is the day to choose life. We must live and allow our babies to live.

May God have mercy on us all.

 # A Personal Testimony

In 1951, I was born into a prominent family. Three years before my birth, my grandfather saw me in a dream. When mother became pregnant, even though she and Dad were very young, my grandfather said that I must be born.

My father Rev. Alfred Daniel Williams King, and mother Naomi King had no idea that they were bringing into the world a child who would one day grow strong and declare an all out war against the Devil. A child who, in 1983, would have a burning desire to help Black men, women and families of different nations to be set free from a system of destruction.

My grandfather, Dr. Martin Luther (Daddy) King, Sr. was a preacher, whereas my uncle (Dad's brother) Dr. Martin Luther King, Jr. was a preacher and a world famous Civil Rights Activist. My Dad was also a preacher and Civil Rights Activist. For many years I longed to capitalize on what I considered to be the fame and accolades that were associated with my uncle during the Civil Rights Movement.

During my lifetime, God blessed me with many abilities. I am the mother of six wonderful children, living today, and three (two aborted, one miscarried) in Heaven. God blessed me to be able to sing, dance and write. I hold several degrees and certificates in Journalism, Business, Counseling, Paralegal, Art, Computers and other skills, such as cooking and gardening. I've been a successful actress and a powerful state legislator. For years, I was greatly self absorbed and overly impressed with myself.

I was in for a very rude awakening in 1983 when I first realized that God wasn't impressed with me. The problem was that I was too much involved with myself and not enough with God. I wanted the spotlight by being recognized for what I considered to be my accomplishments.

In 1983, a colleague of mine at Atlanta Metropolitan College, (where I taught for nineteen years) asked me who was Jesus Christ. Knowing that I had been baptized at the age of five, I really believed that Jesus was born of the Virgin Mary, and that He had died for world on the cross at Calvary. But it's embarrassing to say I didn't know Him. As the colleague began to guide me; through the Scriptures, John 3:16, Roman 1; 10-9, and many others, I realized that there was something missing in my life. I realized that my excursions into Buddhism, Transcendental Meditation, Islam, and other "spiritual" excursions had not provided me with true and complete spiritual guidance. About an hour into our conversation, I realized that Jesus Christ is really the ultimate God, and as I spoke those words aloud, a rushing hunger and desire filled me. I wanted more and more and begin to form an everlasting deep relationship with the Living God. He would become not only a man in a book. He would become my Lord.

I began to be aware of closeness with God that I had never experienced within my entire traumatic life.

To name a few of the tragedies:

1. My baby sister was severely burned when I was five.

2. Our home was bombed in Birmingham, Alabama when we were in bed sleeping during the Civil Rights Movement.

3. I was drugged and arrested for demonstrating during the Civil Rights Open Housing Movement in Louisville. Dad's church was also bombed during this time period.

4. My Uncle Martin (Dad's closest friend) was assassinated.

5. My Dad died mysteriously within months of the assassination.

6. I was married and divorced before I reached the age of 25. I also suffered two abortions during this time period. Abortion was legalized on my birthday in 1973. This was a terrible blow against the civil rights of our youngest and weakest, the babies. I also experienced a miscarriage due to complications arising from the two abortions and use of an IUD. Breast irregularities and cervical problems led to surgery.

7. My dear grandmother was shot and murdered in church while playing the organ.

8. There were always death threats on my whole family.

9. My sister dropped dead while jogging. All of these events occurred prior to 1983.

Since that time:

1. My grandfather who was my closest friend died.

2. My mother's mother died.

3. My brother dropped dead while jogging.

4. I traveled to Europe, Hawaii, The Caribbean Islands, and Mexico.

4. I have almost died several times myself.

5. I have been divorced a third time.

6. I have published several books, produced films and songs, and appeared in movies and television productions.

But there was one major difference. I no longer thought I was the center of my life, and I no longer desired to be recognized as the center of attention. I now realize that it is not about Alveda, it is about God's grace! All that has happened has been either because He was blessing me or delivering me, which is also a blessing. I have experienced witchcraft attacks, physical and emotional abuse, and many traumas, all of which I am convinced, have strengthened me to fight the good fight of faith. Life for me has been exciting with great heights and depths. In my arrogance and ignorance, I grew to believe that the world owed me something because all the wrongs that had been done to me. I was on a disaster course, even though it appeared that I had it all. Then, I met Jesus who brought true joy, meaning and balance to my life. I no longer seek thrills, nor experience great swings from joy to pain. Every moment with Jesus is a joy, even in the midst of trials.

Since 1983, there have been many experiences and events that brought me to this place. I have learned great principles and applied them to my life, since God led me on a path to establish Himself in me.

(1983) I left my political seat at the Georgia Legislature and became a certified paralegal, received my Masters degree in Business, and became a professor. By now, I was a mother of three living and two aborted children.

(1983) I received Jesus as my personal savior.

(1984) I was filled with the Holy Spirit

(1985) a woman whom I have known since my youth came to my rescue when I needed to learn how to protect myself. This special woman taught me how to read the Bible and called upon the name of Jesus. Ephesians 6, The Psalms, especially 91, 37, 23, and 70 were a real blessing to my life. Ecclesiastes, Psalm 139, and the Gospel of John, Esther, all remain my personal favorites. I joined the Fellowship of Faith Church International, and began to learn about Christian warfare.

From there, God led me to a series of good Bible teaching churches. My next child was born.

(1987) God planted me in "Believers' Bible Christian Church" in Atlanta." From 1983 on, I began to see and understand how I had allowed family status, material possessions, worldly fame and other influences to have preeminence in my life. I had looked to humans for answers, while God was there all the time. I had even made my Uncle Martin an idol in my life. I thought that doors would open in the name of Martin Luther King, Jr., even though Martin himself constantly wrote and spoke about the power of God being the solution to all of man's problems. As I began to grow spiritually, I began to want even more of God's power, that authority to overcome life's problems. I no longer wanted to put my confidence in man. I wanted only God who would always protect and nurture me. My next child was born.

(1989) My next child was born.

(1992) I graduated from school of ministry.

(1995) I went to Africa.

(1995) The vision for King for America was birthed. Our mission is to enhance the lives of people spiritually, economically, intellectually and physically. We are a faith based, pro-life, pro-family ministry.

(2002) I became a presidential appointee.

(2004) I became a pastoral associate with Priests for Life.

(2005) King for American launched our film and music vision, with the release of LATTER RAIN and LET FREEDOM RING.

(Today) I am a blessed mother, grandmother and handmaiden of the most High God!

As I continue to grow and learn things of God, I am understanding that we capture the kingdom here on earth with:

1. Knowledge
2. Violence (in the spiritual context, Ephesians. 6: the full armor of God).
3. Money

I began to desire knowledge and money for the right reasons, and to hunger for spiritual authority. What is this Authority? The Pharisees desired to know the same information about Jesus Christ. They asked Jesus, "By what authority do you speak and who gave it to you?" The Pharisees wanted to trick Jesus into claiming that He was God's son. The Pharisees failed to answer Jesus' questions. In turn, Jesus did not answer theirs, which foiled the Pharisees' efforts.

When you try to exercise Kingdom authority with God's permission, your name is likely to be targeted in the book of hell. Satan wants to kill or destroy anyone who realizes who they are in the Kingdom of God. When we know Jesus as our Lord, we no longer have to fear, because we have the whole of Heaven in our corner; the Kingdom of Authority here on earth.

The Kingdom of Authority has always originated from the throne of God, which enables man to have a relationship with God. We must forever honor God, and to hear His instructions.

According to Revelation 12, Satan's plan to overthrow God's kingdom, is defeated, and we bear witness by our presence here on the earth. God used Michael to cast Satan from Heaven to earth. It is critical that we know who we are in Christ Jesus, because once we become aware of our spiritual identities, we should desire things for the right reasons. We should then become more prepared to combat evil.

Let us remain alert to God's resources towards us to further His work here on earth.

In order to know who we are, we must study our presence and heritage in the Bible, in order to see the significant roles God has performed with all of mankind, including the "Black seed." As mentioned previously in this book, our lineage can be traced from Africa during the time of Adam (Eden, and its rivers originated in Africa).

Now since my purpose is firmly established by and with God, my greatest desire is to forgive, be forgiven, to love and grow in God. When we allow Jesus to be the center of our lives, and invite all people to see Him in us, we only help others to know Him intimately. I pray in the name of Jesus that this book in some way, will draw all people unto God (John 3:16).

FOR GOD SO LOVED THE WORLD, THAT HE GAVE HIS ONLY BEGOTTEN SON, JESUS, THAT WHOSOEVER BELIEVES ON HIM, SHALL NOT PERISH, BUT HAVE EVERLASTING LIFE.

2. Freedom to Live: A Pro-Life Perspective from the niece of Dr. Martin Luther King, Jr.

Galatians 4:16 – Have I therefore become your enemy because I tell you the truth?

Jeremiah 22: 3:This is what the Lord says: Do what is just and right. Rescue from the hand of his oppressor the one who has been robbed. Do no wrong or violence to the alien (immigrants), the fatherless (children of single mothers) or the widow, and do not shed innocent blood (murder of the innocents) in this place.

Beyond the boundaries of tradition, our family has always embraced the tenants of the promise of freedom for all people. The Civil Rights Movement of Dr. Martin Luther King, Jr. was birthed from the he Bible, ancient prophecy and New Testament tomes proclaim liberty for captives, freedom from poverty and bondage. Coming from a family of pastors and Bible believing teachers, it is almost natural for one to seek correlations of themes of freedom for everyone, including the pre-born who are often called the unborn and other euphemisms such as fetus, embryo and "blob of tissue."

"And when you discover what you will be in your life, set out to do it as if God Almighty called you at this particular moment in history to do it. Don't just set out to do a good job. Set out to do such a good job that the living, the dead or the unborn couldn't do it any better."

Dr. Martin Luther King, Jr. from Redeeming Lost Values

"I proposed that black churches become central headquarters for a voter drive... We started out with a rally at Ebenezer. Truly, we lived out the word... Walk together children, don't you get weary (words from a Negro spiritual)... Negroes became part of the business of America."

Dr. Martin Luther King, Sr. from DADDY KING

"Some people work so hard a making a living that they forget about how to make a life... We as a race of down-trodden people have been recipients of many good things, yet we have witnessed many, many experiences that were not so favorable... we must work diligently toward a set goal for a better human community here on earth and in the world... I pray God's blessing on you... May we move forward ... with a strong determination to put God first in all that we do, to live in peace and harmony with mankind, and to strive toward making First Baptist Church "God's Little Kingdom Here in Birmingham".

Rev. A. D. Williams King, I

"Abortion is womb lynching."

Dr. Johnny Hunter L.E.A.R.N.

"As a repentant post abortive mother, I boldly proclaim that abortion is not a civil right. Life is a civil right!"

Dr. Alveda King

In the U. S. Constitution, we are taught that all men (human beings) are created equal, and endowed by our Creator with certain unalienable rights to life, liberty and the pursuit of happiness. Our family legacy is rich with the revelation that all men (male and female) includes every human being. This inherent right to liberty comes to all regardless of ethnic persuasion.

God created one race, the human race. (Acts 17:26: "And HE has made from one blood every nation to live on earth.") This is why the scientific find of ancient remains of an African woman called "Eve" traces a DNA/genetic link to every woman living today. We are all one human family, a race my uncle, Dr. King named "the beloved community." This is why the nefarious lie of separate "races" of humans is so dangerous. Race baiting has been allowed to bring divisions to the generations of the human population for far too long.

For those who are research driven, there are many resources that lend insight into the origins of racism. Others shed light on Black/White customs that hinder the development of Dr. King's "beloved community," or what my father termed "God's little kingdom on earth." For starters, see www.answersingenesis.org, www.errvideo.com, www.wallbuilders.com, www.willfordministries.org and read WHO WE ARE IN CHRIST JESUS by Dr. Alveda King.

In his book ONE BLOOD, Ken Ham discusses racism:

"One of the biggest justifications for racial discrimination in modern times is the belief that people groups have evolved separately. Thus, different groups are at allegedly different stages of evolution, and so some people groups are more backward than others. Therefore, the other person may not be as fully human as you. This sort of thinking inspired Hitler in his quest to eliminate Jews and Gypsies and to establish "the master race."

Margaret Sanger, Founder of Planned Parenthood, the world's largest abortion/murder provider, was a contemporary of Hitler, and it is said that she dated one of Hitler's lieutenants.

Sadly, some Christians have been infected with racist thinking through evolutionary indoctrination that people of a different "color" are inferior because they are supposedly closer to the animals. Such attitudes are completely unbiblical (e.g., Acts 17:26, Colossians 3:11), although out-of-context Bible verses are often conscripted in attempts to justify racist views."

In my book WHO WE ARE IN CHRIST JESUS, we consider that since all other races or species of man have either disappeared off the planet, or are in a serious minority, it is evident that the human race is intended to be a family. Because this is a fact that has been established and ordained by God, and since Satan has done everything that he could do to eradicate the family of man, it is no surprise that the wicked old Devil came up with the plan of racism to divide and alienate the populations housed on Planet Earth. Any attempt to deny personhood to any human being is an affront to that person's civil right to live.

At the core of the concept of liberty, justice and freedom is the "personhood" or common humanity of every human being. The Dred Scott decision sought to declare that people of color in America were less than human. In more recent history, Roe versus Wade declared babies in the womb non-persons. In each instance, people were denied their constitutional rights, natural rights, and God given rights to freedom, justice, liberty and the pursuit of happiness.

This is why pro-life, not pro-abortion is a civil right. All people are entitled to freedom to live! Yes, a woman has a right to do what she will with her body. The baby is not her body. Where is the lawyer for the Baby?

The mark of a true civil rights movement in the spirit of Dr. Martin Luther King, Jr. is the foundation of that movement's actions. As a civil rights leader, Dr. King sought prayer, the Bible, and the Church for strength, counsel and direction. Many of the rallies and strategy sessions began in churches across America. The "war songs" are hymns and spirituals and generally Bible based.

"Injustice anywhere is a threat to justice everywhere."

Dr. Martin Luther King, Jr.

The Bible perspective on freedom and liberty allows us to understand that liberty and freedom are God's gift to human beings, and are not to be defined by nor limited by skin color or stages of human development Righteousness and Justice, companions of Liberty and Freedom, are God's vehicles for administering order and fairness to all of his people:

> *Micah 6:8 - What does the Lord require of you but to do justly, To love mercy, And to walk humbly with your God?*

> *Amos 5:24 - Let justice roll on like a river, righteousness like a never-failing stream!*

> *Luke 4:18 - "The Spirit of the Lord is on me, because he has anointed me to preach good news to the poor. He has sent me to proclaim freedom for the prisoners and recovery of sight for the blind, to release the oppressed,*

> *Isaiah 28:17 - I will make justice the measuring line and righteousness the plumb line; hail will sweep away your refuge, the lie, and water will overflow your hiding place.*

> *Leviticus 25:10 - Consecrate the fiftieth year and proclaim liberty throughout the land to all its inhabitants. It shall be a jubilee for you; each one of you is to return to his family property and each to his own clan.*

> *2Corinthians 3:17 - Now the Lord is the Spirit; and where the Spirit of the Lord is, there is liberty.*

Connected to the revelation of the liberty of abundant life is the blessing of purity, marriage and family. Coupled with freedom to live, is freedom to love, marry and procreate.

"The Negro cannot win if he is willing to sacrifice the future of his children for immediate personal comfort and safety."

Dr. Martin Luther King, Jr.

The sanctity of life and the future of our generations are preserved in the institutional commitment of marriage between a man and a woman and the subsequent acts of procreation; the birth and successful rearing of our young. God, the Author of life, grants dominion authority to human beings who desire and accept God's way. In marriage, the divine pattern is for the male to have dominion authority and the woman to have dominion influence. As the two function in concert, order and productivity are established.

At the fall of man, male and female, woman became dissatisfied with her power of influence, and desired male dominion. In contrast, the male, bereft of his authority in the union, became defensive rather than protective. Therefore, the roles of sexuality, intimacy, and compatibility became strained, opening "Pandora's Box" of a multiplicity of acts and behaviors that detract from the original purpose of fruitful multiplication.

Today, in the limited scope of current "liberated" lifestyles, young people are led to believe that sex and marriage between a man and a woman are not sacred and need not be related. The procreative purpose of sexual attraction is secondary, and often nonexistent. Thus contraceptives are used in an attempt to eliminate the opportunity for commitment and permanent bonding. The "anything goes," consequence-free mentality that prevails leads us to a lost generation riddled with emotionally deficient sexual encounters that often lead the participants down a path to multiple sexual encounters, divorce, disease and abortion.

The situation is by no means hopeless. The faithful ranks of "believers" who cling to Christ's tenants of the sanctity of marriage and consequent procreation are being fortified by a new breed of young "survivors" who are committed to purity, Christian courtship, marriage, and the subsequent blessings of rearing their children. Courtships, as in non-sexual romantic activity, can lead to marriage. Dating often leads to sexual encounters without lasting commitment.

If men and women come to understand Divine Purpose for Man (Male and Female), with Male operating in Divine Authority and Female operating in Divine Influence, coupled together in marriage to produce strong babies who grow into strong men and women, the reality of abundant life increases. Too long have women competed with men in an attempt to wrest authority from the spiritual head. Too long have men failed to love and nurture the grace, influence and beauty of the women who were sent to be their "helpmeets". Of course, righteousness (obedience) to God's will is paramount in this equation. With Christ as the head of every relationship, then men and women are free to live abundantly.

As a mother, minister and family relationships counselor, I have experienced an increasingly favorable response to the growing movement to encourage abstinence, chastity, sexual purity, and marriage. As community activists - community servant leaders, as it were - we have a responsibility to lead by example, to teach, and to equip our communities with tools and information that will allow them to succeed in implementing action plans that foster healthy lifestyles.

> *I Corinthians 6: 18 Flee from sexual immorality...*
> *19... Your body is a temple of the Holy Spirit, who is*
> *in you, whom you have received from God? You are*
> *not your own; 20 you were bought at a price. Therefore*
> *honor God with your body.*

May the reading of this chapter bring thoughtful reflection on the topics discussed herein.

3. Exposing the Enemy

Nonviolence is the answer
to the crucial political and moral questions of our time:
the need for man to overcome oppression and violence
without resorting to oppression and violence.
Man must evolve from all human conflict
to a method which rejects revenge, aggression and retaliation.
The foundation of such a method is love.

- Dr. Martin Luther King, Jr. Nobel Peace Prize acceptance speech,
Stockholm, Sweden, December 11, 1964

Man was born into barbarism
when killing his fellow man
was a normal condition of existence.
He became endowed with a conscience.
And he has now reached the day
when violence toward another human being
must become as abhorrent as eating another's flesh.

- Dr. Martin Luther King, Jr.
Why We Can't Wait, 1963

"The most successful, educational appeal to the Negro is through a religious appeal. We do not want word to go out that we want to exterminate the Negro population, and the minister is the man who can straighten out that idea if it ever occurs to any of their rebellious members."

- Margaret Sanger

Some may be surprised that I say my uncle Dr. Martin Luther King, Jr. would be pro-life today. They might point out that he accepted the Margaret Sanger Award from Planned Parenthood, the nation's largest abortion provider. Why would he have done this, if his beliefs were pro-life? Before I answer this, let's go back and take a look at the organization and its founder, Margaret Sanger.

The pseudo-science of eugenics, a forerunner of today's Culture of Death, emerged in the 19th century. Its philosophy could be summed up in the words of Planned Parenthood founder Margaret Sanger, "More children from the fit, less from the unfit."

Underpinning the eugenics attack on the "unfit" was the work of philosopher Thomas Malthus, who developed theories on population growth and economic stability.

To put it mildly, Malthus's views on morality and humanitarian compassion were a far distant cry from the teachings of Dr. Martin Luther King, Jr., who was a Minister of the Gospel of Jesus Christ.

In "An Essay on the Principle of Population," Malthus wrote:

All children born, beyond what would be required to keep up the population to a desired level, must necessarily perish... we should facilitate... the operations of nature in producing this mortality.

Margaret Sanger was an avid follower of Malthus. She embraced his view that the poor and the weak should be purged from the human race to maintain order. Her concept of compassion is embodied in her famous quote, "The most merciful thing a large family can do to one of its members is to kill it."

Sanger, in *The Pivot of Civilization*, called for the elimination of what she called "human weeds," the cessation of charity, the segregation of "morons, misfits, and the maladjusted," and the sterilization of "genetically inferior races." In her periodicals, Sanger also published the writings of those who endorsed the euthanasia, sterilization, abortion, and infanticide programs of Hitler's Third Reich.

In 1921, Sanger founded the Birth Control League, which would later morph into Planned Parenthood. Over the years, her organizations would target black communities for birth control programs. Part of that targeting was a concerted effort to recruit prominent African Americans to endorse birth control.

Uncle Martin was among this select group of leaders, hand picked to promote a seemingly beneficial plan to promote healthy family planning. Unfortunately, it was a plan of wolf-in-sheep's-clothing and Trojan horse proportions. Dr. King, a man of love, peace, non-violence and strong Christian faith, would be assassinated before the truth of the Planned Parenthood map for genocide would be made public after the passage of Roe v. Wade.

On May 5, 1966, Martin Luther King, Jr. became the first person to receive the Planned Parenthood Federation of America's Margaret Sanger Award – the federation's most prestigious honor. In his acceptance speech, Dr. King pointed to the benefits of family planning among African American families and the "kinship" between the civil rights movement and Margaret Sanger's early efforts. With admiration for the founder of the international family planning movement, Dr. King said, "Our sure beginning in the struggle for equality by non-violent direct action may not have been so resolute without the tradition established by Margaret Sanger and people like her."

As Dr. King's niece, I can imagine why he accepted the award. I, too, once accepted the lies of Planned Parenthood. I believed that their carefully crafted public relations façade was real; that they wanted to help me. I even succumbed to abortions until the truth of the violence of abortion was revealed to me.

When Uncle Martin accepted the Sanger Award, pre-Roe liberal state abortion laws had not yet been enacted. In fact, abortion remained illegal during his entire lifetime. Planned Parenthood's eugenic past was not widely known. I know in my soul that if Planned Parenthood had announced in 1966 that over 40 million babies would be aborted in the onslaught of their agenda, Dr. King would never have accepted that award.

The key to my Uncle Martin's heart on the matter of abortion is found in his words. He stated plainly that the Negro could not win by taking the lives of innocent children.

Family planning seems harmless enough. Dr. King supported such a concept. Yet, in his acceptance speech before Planned Parenthood, he spoke of non-violent action. Abortion is very violent to the mother and the child, bearing the poison fruit of death, with links to breast and cervical cancer, emotional sickness, and many other virulent evils. The abortion agenda is in direct conflict with his teachings.

So when people ask me, "What's up with Dr. King's acceptance of the Planned Parenthood award?" my answer can only be that he was sold a bill of goods. A man who spoke out against infanticide would not knowingly support an organization that defended the modern form of infanticide, partial-birth abortion.

In the name of Jesus, I expose the lie of Planned Parenthood, cancel and sever its devious connections with my people, and call upon all people of goodwill to examine the motives and the fruit of its actions.

4. Revelation of the Love of God

"For God so loved the world, that He gave His only begotten Son, that whosoever believes on Him, shall not perish, but shall have everlasting life." John 3:16

God is the author of life.

Life is precious to Him! And each life is precious because we are made in His image.

It's because we are His work that I am moved to work, so that lives might be saved. It's because I am His child that I am moved to urge you to repent and believe, that your soul may be saved.

We don't find God so much as He reveals Himself to us. Through this revelation, He shows His love.

The revelation of the love of God is not about being kind, although being kind comes along with God's love. It is not about being emotional. The love of God is wrapped up in the reality of the Lordship of Jesus Christ.

The love of God was revealed to the Apostle John. Through the Book of John, God will reveal His love to you! You will have to go deep to find it. The Bible says to seek the Lord with all your heart.

The Word also says to love the Lord with all your heart, your soul, your mind, and your strength. Can you truly say that you are doing this today? Are you really after seeing the love of God manifested in your life?

Love God with all of your being. Love other people like you love yourself. Jesus said that these are the most important commandments. In the gospels of Matthew, Luke and John, we see where Jesus first met John. James and John were fishermen with Peter. John caught the greatest revelation of the love of God in his walk with Jesus. The life that Jesus lived, never straying from God's will no matter what anyone did or said to him, affected John. John made a decision to live with this reality in his own life.

In the book of John, chapter one, he wrote, "In the beginning was the Word, and the Word was with God, and the Word was God." Now, centuries after John wrote these words, the eternal Word of God is full of life for us today.

Consider the pro-life message, a message of life and God's redeeming love:

God said: "Today I put before you blessings and curses, life and death, choose life."

Jesus said: I am come that they have life, and have it more abundantly.

And, **Jesus** said: "I am the way, and the truth, and the life...."

John the Baptist, in the womb of his mother Elizabeth, leaped for joy in the presence of his cousin **Jesus,** Who was in the womb of His Mother, Mary.

Let's picture ourselves in the Apostle John's position as a young man. Young folks like to know and experience everything. John traveled with Jesus, asked Him questions, and heard Him daily. Now, if we as Christians can catch hold of what John was saying, that Jesus is the only begotten Son of God, the living Word, with God, is God, we come to see that the Word is the personality that speaks the Word. That makes Jesus and what He says the same. What He says will never pass away. He is still upholding all things by the power of His Word.

Jesus' relationship with God is so much more than just our awareness that he was born of the virgin, His mother, Mary. Jesus lived among humanity. He died for us, went to hell and defeated Satan. Jesus is in Heaven right now, as our High Priest, our Intercessor. He sent the Holy Spirit of God to be with us until His return.

The miracles, like turning the water into wine, giving sight to the blind, healing the crippled, how awesome it must have been to witness them. How would you feel having lived with someone who raised people from the dead? Someone who walked on water? Caused demons to depart?

John had the awesome experience of knowing Jesus. Really knowing Jesus. Not a religious experience, a real experience. There is something in John's little book that will affect your life! In the life and testimony of John, God is giving us the revelation of Jesus, a man who was also God, who defied the powers of that age. The Pharisees and the government couldn't contain Him. Yet, who can contain the Love of God?

There was no question in John's mind that Heaven exists; that the devil is real. These issues are debated in the minds of people today because they do not have the revelation that John had.

John knew that when eternity said, "roll the stone away," a miracle would occur. John knew that He who set time into existence could call Lazarus forth. John left us the roadmap in his first letter:

"That which was from the beginning, which we have heard, which we have seen with our eyes, which we have looked upon, and our hands have handled, of the Word of life...."

Yes, John knew that he had handled the Love of God, the living Word of God revealed:

For the life was manifested, and we have seen it, and bear witness, and show unto you that eternal life, which was with the Father, and was manifested unto us.

Yes, the Love of God can be manifested if you have the heart to receive it! John did. Do you?

That which we have seen and heard declare we unto you, that you also may have fellowship with us; and truly our fellowship is with the Father, and with His Son Jesus Christ. And these things we write unto you, that your joy may be full.

Is your joy full today? If so, glory be to God. Pass it on. If not, keep pressing on. This love is available to you! This is not just a religious saying. This is not a storybook tale. You can know the love of God!

John had face to face encounters with the Love of God! Jesus looked like a man, but He was so much more outstanding! John was allowed to go to the Mount of Transfiguration with Jesus. After that experience, John was even more convinced that Jesus could accomplish whatever He desired. John understood that Jesus controlled the armies of the world. John understood that all power belonged to Christ. John said he'd looked upon Him, handled the Words of Life! Get this, now. Here is a being in a physical body, yet John knew that he'd had the occasion to touch He who had framed the world and all creation. John is speaking from experience. He is saying that he had the occasion to witness the Son of God free a woman bent with infirmity for eighteen years. John saw Jesus speak and saw the woman's body completely restored. Would you say that that woman's joy was full after that?

This reality became such a part of John, that they couldn't kill him. The other apostles died as martyrs, but not John. History has it that they even tried to boil him in oil, and it didn't hurt him. What a revelation of the power of the love of God!

Jesus said, "I am come that they may have life, and have it more abundantly." Man did not have abundant life. He'd lost it in the Garden of Eden. Jesus brought it all back to us. Think about it. God told Adam that once he'd partaken of that tree, he'd surely die. Death then came into the world. Subsequently, thousands of years later, after all kinds of deaths and curses, John lived to see Love in action. John saw Love alive! John touched and handled the Love of God! So can you! Can you handle it! More importantly, do you want to handle it? Do you want to touch and feel the Jesus that John knew?

You must be aware that you don't have to be denomination minded. You don't have to be church minded! You don't have to be church duty minded. When you serve God with all of your heart, your mind, your soul, serving the eternal, everlasting Word of God -- then you are on the road to Love that John knew.

Think about this, now. We as Christians are about the only group who doesn't major in what we believe. Athletes major in sports. Singers major in singing. We can get to know mathematics, computers, and mechanics. Most of us are up on some subject because we have applied ourselves to coming to know it. People even major in serving idols and the devil. Yes, we approach these kinds of things with an attitude of mastering them, so we succeed.

Yet, we Christians are just failing when it comes to spiritual things. In our knowledge and use of spiritual things, we don't even know two plus two equals four. If the Church were a learning institution, most Christians would get failing grades. We get after kids for playing hooky, yet we play spiritual hooky all the time. The professor is in class, the students don't show up. The things we should know most of all, we know least of all. The spiritual things that directly affect our lives simply escape most of us.

We are not like John. We've not had that spiritual experience, of handling the Word of life. We want to treat preachers like doctors. We think we don't have to know what doctors know or use what doctors use to get well. We just expect the doctor to perform and we'll just sit there and get better without really understanding why. Yet the Bible says, "My people perish for lack of knowledge." You need to have the knowledge that the Word is giving you.

You need to know where your healing is and your right standing with God is. You need to know the assistance of angelic forces you have. But most of us don't have this, so life remains a mystery to us. We fail to comprehend spiritual things. This is one of the most disheartening things for a minister of the gospel. You see that people are not equipped, and they won't try to get it. It's like never learning how to count, or even what money is, and then going to the grocery store and having the clerk ask you for twenty dollars. You don't know what twenty dollars is. You never took the time to find out how to count. You are lost.

How many Christians know how to cook better than they know God? God should be above everything else that we know. One day, you'll come face to face with the reality that you need to know your Savior. When that day comes, if you don't know Him, it will almost be like trying to get somebody to breathe for you, or to get his or her heart to beat for you. It won't work. You must know this reality for yourself. You must personally know your God.

This is what John is talking about. We must have this same kind of experience, this Truth. When you are living every day, the Word of God should be just as real in everything you do as when you open your Bible and read it. You need to pray and ask God to reveal His Word to you -- not just as book knowledge, but as it applies in your everyday life. When you ask God to reveal His Word to you, allow Him to do it. Then, live the Word, do the Word! From Genesis One to the last page of Revelation, the Word of God should be real to you. The fall and redemption of man should be just as real to you as breathing.

You need to know that God is involved in your life. You are a product of the plan and purpose of God! His Love is higher than anything you can ever comprehend. You are a member of the family, the kingdom of God. You are of God, little children. He is your Abba Father, your Daddy.

We can have racial differences, social differences, and lack of associations. Christianity brings us together, or at least it should. You know why this hasn't happened? There's not enough revelation of the Love of God in the Church. When you see yourself more than you can see God, you don't have a revelation of God. When it's all about "my organization, my plan, my, my, my," then there is no victory.

When you don't have a revelation of God, it is easy to turn a blind eye to the way to end abortion. When you can see yourself and your own agenda and you're missing the picture of the gifts in the people around you, you're not seeing God, the Father, Son and Holy Spirit.

The revelation of the Love of God should be growing in your life every single hour, day, and year. There should be a depth of the reality and application of this love that wasn't there last year. You have to get your purpose, which is to be fulfilled in the love of God! You might want to start by majoring in First John. Once you get a handle on that, you can go on to learn the character of Love in First Corinthians 13. Don't jump ahead of yourself, thinking you know algebra when you don't have two plus two down. Touch, handle, and know the love of God for yourself. Love never fails. Even faith works by love!

When we know God, then we are well on the way to victory! Our prayers make it to the Throne of God, and we receive results. We won't get weary in the pro-life battle. We will work together and shoulder the burdens together.

If we allow the powerful love of God to come into our lives to unite us, we can defeat the forces of abortion that are plaguing our people. We can overcome the power of abortion if we unite in love and truth and work together. This way, we will not condemn, we will win over the voices and forces of darkness. We will not condemn the post-abortive parents, the abortion providers, those who are in the camp of abortion. We will pray, we will teach, we will vote, we will march. We will do all that is necessary to win. Most importantly, we will do it God's way, in love.

Now abides faith, hope and love. Yet, the greatest of these is love. Keep yourselves in the love of God, dear ones. May your joy be full, complete and overflowing. Amen.

This chapter was inspired by the teaching of my Mentor, Pastor Allen McNair of Believers' Bible Christian Church in Atlanta, Georgia.

Book Cover

A.D. King Family

Daddy and Mama King Family 1964

A.D. King and Alveda 1969

Brother
to the Dream

Born of a preacher
In the shadow of the dream,
Upholding the plight of the
downtrodden,
Blood brother to Martin,
Brother in spirit to the masses
To know him was to experience
great joy
As he preached in the Word of
our Lord and Savior Jesus Christ,
saying, "peace by still"

Rev. Doctor A. D. Williams King I
1930 - 1969

A.D. King, Daddy King with grandchildren and great grandchildren 1979

March on Washington

A.D. King, John Porter and Nelson Smith pray
in Birmingham, 1963 Easter Black Out

Bombing of A. D. King family parsonage, Birmingham 1963

Uncle Dr. Martin Luther King, Jrn. Funeral 1968

(photos available at www.kingforamerica.com)

State Representative Alveda King, 1983

Alveda for Congress with mother, Naomi King 1983

Acts 17: Of one blood, God created all people

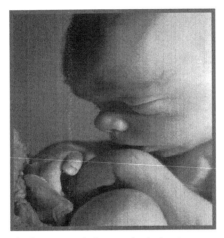

4d ultra sound-6 months baby in utero

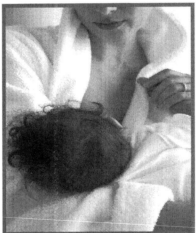

9 months baby with mother

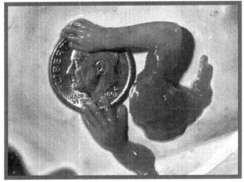

6 months baby aborted
(photos available at www.priestsforlife.org)

48

5.　We All Have A Voice

In this section of the book, various issues are addressed in light of the pro-life message. Often, we don't see the connections between news stories and underlying moral issues. They are definitely related. It is our duty, no matter what our station in life happens to be, to speak out when children are dying.

I invite you to speak out more in your own communities. Use your voice in your own circles of influence! Speak out at home, at church, at community events. Organize prayer circles. Get on the radio! Write editorials. You may ask: "Who? Me?" The answer is, "Who else?"

In this first article, an appeal was made to African-American leaders to become involved in the civil rights cause of our time, equal protection for the unborn. Since the letter was written, the Southern Christian Leadership Conference, and the National Association for the Advancement of Colored People have revisited the pro-life issue. All across America, leaders of every ethnic group, every religious denomination, every socio-economic status are hearing the cries of the babies .We can attribute this "change of heart" to the combined efforts of prayer and action on the parts of countless of pro-life warriors, some of whom we may never meet.

AN OPEN LETTER
TO AFRICAN-AMERICAN LEADERS
June 2006

This is an open letter to appeal to all people who respect the work, life and teachings of Dr. Martin Luther King, Jr. More specifically, it is a wake-up call to the African American community. As a mature, Black, female living in America, my heart weeps every time I hear or see stories about our youth cut down in acts of senseless violence. Time after time, I have asked the question, HOW CAN THE DREAM SURVIVE IF WE MURDER THE CHILDREN?

In America, we have unleashed a culture of death, and our children are dying. Every day, there are stories across our land of children committing violent acts against themselves, other children and adults. Because we have committed over 40 million legal murders in our recent history, our children can't discern between what is good, what is legal and what is right.

Please carefully consider the missions of two of our most prominent Civil Rights organizations, the SCLC and the NAACP, and the words of a noted African-American leader.

National Association for the Advancement of Colored People Mission Statement: "To ensure the political, educational, social and economic equality of rights of all persons and to eliminate racial hatred and racial discrimination."

Southern Christian Leadership Conference: "We are recommitting ourselves to advocating and teaching the principles of nonviolence taught by Dr. King… to provide people with viable alternatives to solving their problems without resorting to violence."

Tavis Smiley: "The Covenant with Black America is a national plan of action to address the primary concerns of African Americans today".

Here, we nobly speak of the equality of rights for all persons, action plans and non-violent solutions, while the rights of the helpless and the pre-born are continually violated in often the most violent acts imaginable. Indeed, in America, since 1973, over 40 million American babies have been legally murdered. At least 13 million of these babies were Black. Two of these babies were mine. Coupled with the blatant practice of euthanasia, and the open assault on marriage and family, we have lost and continue to lose millions of our children in this culture of death. Some may argue that a woman has a right to chose what she does with her body. She does, but where is the lawyer for the baby, who is like a helpless slave in the womb of his/her mother?

This letter is an open appeal to all people of good will, and today, especially to African-American leaders, to stop the violence, to save the children, to restore the culture of life to America.

Please respond to the voices of the children! Visit our website today, to sign up to make a difference. It's www.priestsforlife.org/africanamerican. We would love to meet with you, to hear your heart on this vital issue. God bless you.

Yours for Life,

Dr. Alveda C. King, Pastoral Associate

As I wrote earlier in this book, we seem to be suffering from a logical and moral disconnect in our society. One of my goals is to correct these maladies by discussing connections between the "what" and the "why" of news stories.

The following are press releases I've issued to point out what I believe is the root cause of much of the violence, pain, and disregard for human life we see everyday in our nation. That root cause is the Culture of Death spawned by abortion on demand.

Dr. Alveda King Says Hilton and Wilson Cases Linked by a 'Consequence-Free' Mindset

Washington, DC – Dr. Alveda King, Pastoral Associate of Priests for Life, today commented on an issue raised by the criminal cases of Genarlow Wilson, a man sentenced to ten years of prison at the age of 17 for having criminal consensual sex with a 15-year-old girl, and socialite Paris Hilton.

"On the surface, there's nothing similar about the cases of Genarlow Wilson and Paris Hilton," said Dr. King, niece of the late Dr. Martin Luther King, Jr. "One would be hard pressed to immediately see a link between the two and I wouldn't presume to comment on the details or merits of either person's situation, but from a distance, they seem to be examples of an attitude that's at the root of many of society's problems. Too many of us feel we can do what we know is wrong and not have to face the consequences of our actions."

"I believe that a generation's having grown up with legal abortion is a big reason for the consequence-free mindset that plagues our young; after all, if a culture says you can kill a baby to 'fix' unwanted pregnancy, how serious could it be to deal with other problems you cause? We need to pray for our children. We need to monitor the media they absorb. And we need to teach them – if you want to avoid the rude awakening of painful consequences, don't do what's 'right for you,' do what's right."

Dr. Alveda King to Congressman Rangel: "Save the Babies, Save Social Security"

Washington, DC – Dr. Alveda King, Pastoral Associate of Priests for Life, today responded to reports that Congressman Charles Rangel, Chairman of the House Ways and Means Committee, is working on a plan to save Social Security from a coming financial crunch.

"Congressman Rangel has to be aware that since the Roe v. Wade decision in 1973, approximately 48 million Americans, about a third of them African Americans, have been aborted," said Dr. King, the niece of the late Dr. Martin Luther King, Jr. "Millions of those now deceased people would have been alive and paying into Social Security today had not Mr. Rangel and his friends in the abortion lobby had their way. It's time Mr. Rangel and his fellow Congressmen connect the dots – save the babies, save Social Security."

Dr. Alveda King Says Sen. Obama's
"Quiet Riot" Comment Misses the Point

Washington, DC – Dr. Alveda King, Pastoral Associate of Priests for Life and niece of the Rev. Martin Luther King, Jr., today responded to the remarks of Senator Barack Obama, who said that "quiet riots" take place in black neighborhoods every day because of hopelessness.

"Senator Obama may know of the 'quiet riots' coming from the black community," said Dr. King, "but he doesn't understand their source. Seventeen million black babies have been killed by abortion and the cries of those children, their mothers, and their families are what Senator Obama is hearing. I invite him to listen to those cries more clearly and compassionately. I pray he will realize that hopelessness and despair are only deepened by aborting those who are the future."

Concerning the Comments of Talk Show Host Don Imus – A Statement by Dr. Alveda King

Atlanta, GA – The racist slurs hurled by radio host Don Imus are reprehensible and certainly warrant the outrage that has followed. The fact that certain black men use similar or identical words when talking about black women is not a defense for Mr. Imus's epithets, only further evidence of the debasing of American culture.

The Imus scandal highlights a deeper and broader problem in our country, the disrespect we have for each other. The murders of my father, the Rev. A.D. King, and my uncle, Dr. Martin Luther King, were born of this disrespect. So were the deaths of 48 million babies by abortion. When we regard certain people as lesser than ourselves, the value of life is cheapened.

To me, it's as offensive to call an unborn baby a "blob of tissue" as it is to call a black woman a "ho." The disrespect to humanity is the same. My outrage is the same.

Yes, Don Imus's apologies are necessary. But I demand the same from every public figure who has ever said that babies in the womb are not persons.

Statement by Alveda King on the
Extension of the Voting Rights Act

July 27, 2006

The right to vote has always been fundamental in America, yet it took years of struggle and sacrifice before that right was extended to everyone in this country. I am intimately familiar with that struggle and sacrifice.

While I am thrilled that the right to vote will continue to be guaranteed by the Voting Rights Act, I am grieved that another fundamental right has not yet been extended to everyone in this country - the right to life. As a post-abortive mother and Pastoral Associate at Priests for Life, I am intimately familiar with the struggle and sacrifice to extend this right, as well.

African Americans comprise 12 percent of this nation's population, yet 32 percent of the babies aborted in the United States are black. To put it bluntly, abortion is doing what those who lynched and bombed and burned could not - it is taking away the God given rights of African Americans and everyone else who society today doesn't wish to recognize as equals.

Discrimination and violence against the weak and voiceless of all colors and ethnicities continue in the form of abortion, but they must and will end.

I sincerely thank President Bush for his support of the Voting Rights Act. And I bless him for supporting the right to life of all of God's children.

Dr. Alveda King on New Crime Statistics: We Have Sown the Wind of Death in Abortion Clinics and Reaped the Whirlwind of Violence in Our Streets

Atlanta, GA – Dr. Alveda King, Pastoral Associate of Priests for Life and the niece of Rev. Martin Luther King, Jr., today reacted to the release of new Department of Justice crime statistics showing African Americans to be the victims of nearly half of the murders committed in 2005.

"That 49 percent of all Americans murdered are black is shocking," said Dr. King. "That 93 percent of those people are victims of black on black crime is not really surprising. The abortion industry has told African Americans for decades that killing our own children is beneficial, even therapeutic. We bought their lies and life in the inner city has become cheap."

"You want another shocking statistic?" asked Dr. King. "Black women are now three times more likely to abort than white women. Yes, 8,000 African Americans were murdered by guns and knives in 2005, but hundreds of thousands more were terminated by more socially acceptable weapons. We have sown the wind of death in abortion clinics and reaped the whirlwind of violence in our streets."

"The killing has to stop," declared Dr. King. "If we are to restore our communities and our families, respect for individuals has to begin when their lives begin, in the womb."

Vick Dog Fighting Scandal "Reminds Me of Other Cruelty" Says Dr. Alveda King

Atlanta, GA – Dr. Alveda King, Pastoral Associate of Priests for Life and niece of Dr. Martin Luther King, Jr., today said that the allegations of animal cruelty announced in the case against star quarterback Michael Vick highlight the disparity in societal protections for animals and unborn humans.

"The appalling cruelty to dogs described in the complaint against Michael Vick immediately reminds me of another kind of cruelty that is not only not punished, but is protected by our authorities," said Dr. King. "I'm talking about the incredible cruelty suffered by babies who are stabbed, have limb torn from limb, or have their skulls crushed in the womb by abortionists. The pain these children endure is undoubtedly excruciating, yet we close our eyes and look the other way in the name of 'choice.'"

"Yes, of course we should ensure humane treatment of animals," said Dr. King, "but shouldn't we also humanely treat humans?"

Jena Six Case Highlights Need to Investigate Evidence of Racism Everywhere, Including the Abortion Industry, Says Dr. Alveda King

Atlanta, GA – Dr. Alveda King, Pastoral Associate of Priests for Life and niece of the late Dr. Martin Luther King, Jr., commented today on the Jena Six case in Louisiana, where six African American high school students involved in a fight with white students have been charged with crimes that could send them to prison for decades. Critics of the prosecutions, citing racial segregation at the school and discriminatory prosecution of only the black students involved in the fight, are asking the Justice Department to investigate.

"The call to investigate the Jena Six prosecutions is legitimate," said Dr. King. "There's clear evidence in the case that officials need to examine for discriminatory practices, from the nooses strung from a tree that helped provoke the fight to the vast difference in the severity of treatment given to white and black participants."

"There's other evidence of racism in our nation, though, that also troubles me to the core and that also demands investigation," added Dr. King. "The abortion industry kills black babies at an alarmingly high and disproportionate rate, it situates its clinics primarily in minority neighborhoods, and it has eliminated one-quarter of the African American population. Abortionists don't wear hoods, but one has to wonder how the results of the abortion industry's practices would be much different if they did. Black babies are being denied their fundamental right to live and it's time to find out why the people who profit from abortion in this country seem to be targeting African Americans."

6.   Abortion Is Not A Civil Right!

In this section, various life related issues are addressed. This portion of the book is intended to stimulate thought, and inspire the reader to conduct further research.

LIFE IS A CIVIL RIGHT!

Prior to the Civil Rights movement of the 1960s, people were being oppressed due to God given skin color. They were denied rights such as the right to vote, to live where they wanted, or to use public facilities, all because of something over which God, not they, had control.

Today, people are being oppressed, again because of who they are. Life in the womb is God ordained. We don't choose to be conceived any more than we choose our skin color. In a free society, people should not be persecuted because of their age or size any more than they should be persecuted because of their race.

Our Declaration of Independence says that each of us is granted the rights to life, liberty, and the pursuit of happiness by our Creator. Justice demands that our government acknowledge and protect these rights, especially the foremost one, the right to life.

A WOMAN HAS A RIGHT TO CHOOSE WHAT SHE DOES WITH HER BODY, BUT THE BABY IS NOT HER BODY!

To be fair about it, we must admit that a woman has a right to choose what she does with her own body. This right is not absolute, though. In most jurisdictions, a woman has no right to engage in prostitution or illicit drug use. With regard to abortion, the right is irrelevant. A baby, while inside and connected to a woman's body, is not part of her body. Science proves that the baby has DNA distinct from his or her mother's. The child is a separate, living human being and, as such, has as much claim to equal protection as the mother.

THE WOMB IS MEANT TO BE A SANCTUARY, NOT A TOMB.

Think about it. A sanctuary is a place of safety and shelter. When a child is aborted a violent act occurs, not just to the child, but to the mother. Abortion is very violent and very invasive. The sanctuary of the womb is violated. Later, when other babies are conceived in that same womb, they must live for nine months in a place where their sibling was violently murdered. Is there any wonder that the mother/child bond is affected.

THE BABY IN THE WOMB IS LIKE A SLAVE.

Consider this. During the first days of American history, black people were slaves. They were not considered human. Their slave masters could feed them, clothe them, house them, and nurture them. Or they could beat them and kill them. At will. The same is true of a preborn baby. The baby is so dehumanized that he or she is not even called human. The labels embryo and fetus are meant to deny humanity. A baby in the womb is a human being, with the same rights to life, liberty and the pursuit of happiness that we all have.

ABORTION IS NEVER JUST ABOUT THE MOTHER.

Abortion wounds the mother. It kills the baby. Abortion also kills the father's child, the grandparents' grandchild, the son's brother, the daughter's sister, the uncle's niece, the aunt's nephew, the adoptive parents' child to be adopted, and on and on. Have you ever seen "It's a Wonderful Life"? Have you ever wondered what life would be like if someone you now love had been aborted? And have you ever wondered what wonderful people the world has lost because they were terminated before they could take their first breaths?

INJUSTICE ANYWHERE IS A THREAT TO JUSTICE EVERYWHERE.

The words of Dr. Martin Luther King, Jr. ring with truth. Abortion is the intentional killing of a human being. Because of no act of his or her own, the innocent baby is forced to die. Here in America, the land of the "free," the helpless are being slaughtered in the name of "choice." What could be more unjust? Today, we talk about fighting for the culture of life against the culture of death. What we have right now is a culture of sin. Forty-five million Americans are missing, all of them victims of injustice. The ramifications of this can't possibly end on the clinic table.

SURVIVORS AND OVERCOMERS.

We are all survivors. Think about it, our parents didn't abort us. Anyone born after Roe v. Wade knows this all too well. Post-abortive parents who have sought and found forgiveness are overcomers.

Women who give birth to their babies in the face of pressure to abort are both survivors and overcomers.

CONCEPTION DAY VERSUS BIRTHDAY.

In China, conception day is celebrated with as much, if not more fanfare than birthdays receive around the world. My birthday is January 22. I was conceived in May. I celebrate both, with more emphasis on conception. This is a way of bringing attention to the humanity of all people. When we acknowledge that a baby is a human being from the moment of conception, then we truly embrace Dr. King's beloved community.

THE PRO-CHOICE LOBBY –
MODERN DAY PHAROAHS.

In Atlanta, Georgia, people visit the tomb of Dr. Martin Luther King, Jr. Dr. King was often considered to be a modern day Moses. When Moses was born, the genocide of his times sought to kill all the baby boys of his nation to prevent the liberation of a people. The midwives, though, refused to kill or abort the babies. Today, there are battles in state legislatures to help doctors, nurses, and pharmacists make the same choice for life. But just as Pharoah tried to impose his deadly will, so does the abortion lobby. The pro-choice crowd doesn't want to allow medical professionals any choice at all.

THE ABORTION INDUSTRY IS RACIST

My friend, pro-life advocate Dr. Johnny Hunter, founder of the group LEARN (Life Education and Research Network), says that "abortion is womb lynching. Unlike the KKK, abortionists don't wear hoods, but their form of genocide is more effective than the tactics of the KKK against freed slaves and their descendents."

The facts are plain. Black women are three times more likely to abort than white women. While blacks comprise 12 percent of the American population, we have 35 percent of the abortions. Over three-quarters of Planned Parenthood's clinics are located in minority areas. Coincidence? Hard to believe.

CONSIDER:

Satan hates virgins, thus a sexual revolution
that flies in the face of God!
Behold, a Virgin shall conceive...
Satan hates babies, thus genocide.
JESUS IS LORD OVER ALL! And His Name shall be
called Wonderful, Counselor, The Prince of Peace, The
Everlasting Father, and His Kingdom shall have no end!

ABORTION IS AN ATROCITY AGAINST THE HUMAN RACE!

Acts 17 teaches that we are all of the same blood, the same family. I am evidence of a multi-ethnic humanity. Our family tree includes Africa, Ireland, and Native American ancestry! An even stronger Blood Covenant is the Blood of Jesus. Forty million aborted? Fifty million? Who's counting? God is counting. He's calling us to say enough is enough!

TIME OUT FOR POLITICS.

Tell your candidates that you will no longer vote for murder. God is not a Republican or a Democrat! Voting for what is right is not a question of political loyalty. Try telling God, "I didn't vote for the person who wanted to protect your children because I didn't like his political party." Let's get real about it. Righteousness and Justice belong together (Isaiah 28). Life is a universal human issue, a universal human right.

ABORTION IS A SOCIAL JUSTICE ISSUE!

Who is more oppressed than the baby about to be aborted? He is physically helpless; he's poor, without an income or assets; has no advocate, much less a court appointed attorney; is ignored by the major media, and is not allowed even to be seen by his mother before he's executed. If anyone truly cares about social justice, he has to care about the unborn.

ABORTION IS DANGEROUS!

According to scientific studies, abortion can be a contributing factor to the development of breast cancer, cervical cancer, ovarian cancer, liver cancer, placenta previa, difficulties with subsequent pregnancies, life-threatening ectopic pregnancies, and endometritis. Abortion can result in uterine perforation which in turn can result in hysterectomy, cervical lacerations which can cause long-term reproductive damage, infection, excessive bleeding, embolism, hemorrhage, convulsions, toxic shock, and death. Then there are the emotional and psychological problems....

And they call abortion "safe"?

SOLUTIONS TO ABORTION:

• Education and Information – the Bible says that we shall know the truth, and the truth shall make us free. We must study and learn all that we can and share that knowledge with others.

• Abstinence – Abstinence until marriage is a sure way to avoid pregnancy and abortion. Period. Adultery, fornication, same gender cohabitation are all forms of human sexuality that lead to social and physical problems. Abstinence and celibacy answer these concerns. There are many resources available on how to make abstinence work until you are ready for a family.

•   Mentoring Opportunities – Everyone needs good counsel. Many of us are equipped to mentor, guide and bless. Pray about it, then act.

•   Healing Opportunities – There is healing available for everyone. Post-abortion healing is available online, in your hometown, and always from God!

•   Healthy Crisis Intervention – Pregnancy care centers are opening every day, even as the abortion mills are closing.

•   Values Based Success Mapping – Values for life! Map your own pattern for success, following the paths of life.

LIFE IS A CIVIL RIGHT! CHOOSE LIFE!

7.   Visual Learning and the Culture of Life

"A picture is worth a thousand words."

- Anonymous

"America will not reject abortion until America sees abortion."

-- Frank Pavone

Our learning experiences shape our understanding. They also form our methods of communicating with and relating to others. As a post-abortive mother who has spent over 20 years as an educator, with many of those years spent with young people with me as a classroom teacher, I find it natural to consider learning styles when seeking more effective ways to share the pro-life message.

Learning styles are an integral part of working to share the "culture of life" in every community. Because I am an African-American woman, I am especially interested in reaching the people of my communities.

It has been said that African-Americans have a particular learning style that causes them to be global learners in that they want to see the big picture and not necessarily all the small details. They also tend to be better writers than speakers because they excel in non-verbal communication. In addition, they tend to use approximations frequently and focus better on a person rather than an inanimate object. One of the characteristics of our African-American culture is an emphasis on visual learning. We are particularly impacted by visual imagery.

For many years, I have been an outspoken advocate for the unborn child, because in a culture of abortion, the child is like a slave. The new civil rights movement of our time is the pro-life movement, and as I seek to preserve the dream of my uncle, Dr. Martin Luther King, Jr., and of my father, Rev. A.D. King (Martin's brother), I once again ask the question, "How can the Dream survive if we murder the children?" I grew up watching these two great men fight for the equal rights of their people.

But equality is not something you can see. What you can see are people. My uncle knew that the ugly reality of segregation and discrimination had to be seen visually by the American public. He therefore organized events at which the eyes of the media could broadcast the way our people were treated when water hoses and dogs were unleashed on their peaceful marches. People responded to those images with horror and compassion; not simply as abstract concepts of "segregation" and "equality."

Likewise, people – and especially African Americans – respond to the disturbing images of aborted children. Sure, some people get angry when we show them. But everyone who fights injustice has to be ready to pay a price. My uncle did, and so did my dad. So does everyone who has the courage to show the ugly reality of abortion. Don't be afraid to do so.

As a woman who has had two abortions, I am grateful that the truth is being shown, so that others can avoid this pain in the first place. Remember, people may not want to hear the truth, but when confronted with its image, they can't help but see it. And when they see it, it becomes harder to deny.

8. Selected Poetry by Alveda King

For Generations To Come

Our family tree
means more to me, Than silver
or gold, or a
Rolls Royce.

I can rejoice and be glad,
that Mother and Dad, loved each other
- and GOD
Who blessed their union.

From one to another, we ate linked
to each other...
Through the blessings and mercy of our awesome
CREATOR

Our Creator, the Artist, Who reminds us of
ETERNITY

In the smiles of our children, who have the
Spirit of our ancestors-
Twinkling out from their eyes...

Reminding us
of
GENERATIONS to COME.

SJ Forevermore

SJ, today
You lift me up.

Yesterday, you filled my cup.
Tomorrow and forevermore,
You are my keys to Heaven's door.

Praise to
Father
Son
and Spirit.
Thanks, S.J.,
Forevermore.

P.S. Thanks for breaking bonds and curses.
Sunshine feels real good.

Politics Can Make You...

Mad
Powerful
Excited
Politics can shape you, Politics can break you
Politics can woo you - to spend and WIN
Politics can make you. GOD, Don't let it TAKE you
Body
Soul
Spirit
or politics can make you
a political animal.

Money

Don't tell me that money is the root of all evil. That may be so. Sometimes I feel that the White man, knowing that Blacks (having no want to be evil) would believe the myth that the possession of money can cause evil deeds. However, lack of money causes much more evil situations, like little children with sagging skin and swollen bellies; families living in matchbox houses, literal fire traps; victims of poverty forced to steal because they feel there is no other way.

Yes, I like money. Not only because it can buy things for me, but because one day, if I get enough money, I can help others.

There is one class in our society who thinks more about money than the rich, and they are the poor. They can think of nothing else, which is the misery of being poor. Poverty produces degradation.

For me, money will always be an instrument to be handled, a weapon to fight poverty - not a deity to be worshiped.

Voices

You gave life voice
    To sing sweet psalms.

Life sings of degradation.

    You gave life ears to hear
your music

Life listens to pagan drums.

Life has many voices Lord.
    We need to only listen.

Of all the voices in my life
    Yours is sweetest.

Where Is Passion?

We crave a passion, hot and burning
We long for love, forever yearning

Our flesh deceives us, our loins mislead us
The path of throbbing passion calls us

Where is the joy of love? Nay, lust
leaves us crawling in the dust

Panting, wanting, needing, pleading
Forever searching, not succeeding.

Until submission, sure and lasting,
leads us to the source of power.

Power, pleasure, joy; Yes Passion;
Wait for us behind the door. When we yield
We know forever, love yes love,

Forevermore.

Ripples (In Time And Space)

Libations, fluids rippling on the sands bringing time and space
together; Bringing souls and spirits together... pebbles on the water,
water making ripples,
Ripples in time.
"Behold I show you a mystery; We shall not all sleep, but we shall all
be changed
In a moment, in the twinkling of an eye, at the last trump;
For the trumpet shall sound, and the dead shall be raised
Incorruptible
And we shall be changed."

II

Libations, shadows rippling on the sand
The earth beneath my feet changes from my dark and musky
Mother, becoming red and alien, harsh,
As the waters ripple and the great ship rolls.

III

I am carried away from my familiar jungle of fruits and passion flowers,
wild
animal friends and even wilder beasts;
Four legged animals, predators and yet, magnificent creations of God,
with
skins and furs ...and fangs.

IV

Yet, change carries us over waters that no longer
Ripple.
The water becomes an awesome, rolling jungle of waves
That carries us on in the Middle Passage
Washing us away from our home ground to a new land of tears and
sorrow,
Our newfound home in a new world.

V

And yet, wherever we were bought,
Beaten and scattered, over continents and islands,
New blood was added to our veins; and yet the Blood of our
Motherland remained,
True and deep.
In our new world, we learned to harvest new crops;
Some not quite so different from our jungle fruits and vegetation.
We tamed fields of cotton and tobacco
Even as our wild, free spirits were tamed by the new predator; two-
legged beasts, still creatures of God, and not quite so magnificent in
their borrowed skins and furs. But still their fangs, though changed
remain deadly.

VI

The libations continue;
The spirits that were summoned bring new birth to memories;
Reflections of time itself.
We see ourselves in a new jungle -- still a part of God's creation,
And yet, the earth has changed.
The soil is not dark and musty between our bare and braceleted feet,
Nor is it red and cracked beneath our chained and callous feet.
It has become rock, concrete,
A machine-made improvement on nature,
And yet still part of nature.

VII

The tribal dancers before the sun, the wind, the rain and the Moon
have become whirling disco bodies beneath a myriad of simulated
starlight,
Lightning and thundering electro phonic sounds.

VIII

The hunter's spears and darts have become a mania for Money;
And guns bring down men and prey upon the weak who become
Homeless, Jobless, and
Dreamless.

IX

The savagery continues, though times and methods change. The lie
of racism causes us to forget that we are all of one blood. Slaughter
begins in the womb, and the terror rains down across the ages.
Humanity seems to have forgotten why we are here.

Humankind has changed, and yet has not changed, only
Shimmered and rippled in the reflections of time.

X

For though one generation passeth away, another generation cometh.
As the sun rises, it sets only to rise again.
The wind goes to the south only to return to the north,
Whirling continually, returning again according to its circuits.
And the rivers run to the sea, yet the sea is not full,
For the rivers return again to that place from which they came.
For that which has been, shall be again, and that which has been done,
Shall be done again.
For as all things change, they remain because: "There is no new thing under the sun." There are only rippling images of change, all belonging to the universe, The Old, the New created by the Omnipotent
The Lord GOD! Who changes not,

The Companions

BIG MOMA

It's yo' show, Big Moma.
At least, that's what they call you, ain't it?
With yo' minks, and lynx, and diamond studded sphinx,
You strut round like some reincarnated Nefertiti.
If someone were to ask you bout the Virgin Birth,
(you've given birth, but y'aint no virgin)
Would you say, "VIRGIN?" How unfashionable,
Virgins went out with the bite from that passion fruit, back there.
In the Garden, all those years ago.
Where, in the world,
Can you find a virgin these days?
I sure would like to sink my fangs...
Excuse me. Teeth
Into
A Virgin
Does this turn our mind to blood covenants? Occult violations?
Blood spilled out and sucked up over the centuries.
Blood untold, blood washing away the sins of the world?
The covenant Blood of the LAMB?
Maybe this is a dream. A fantasy.
A motion picture slice from the mind of a dreamer
Seeking eternity in the arms of
Her Savior
Where yo gonna go?
I don't know
It's yo' show,
Big Moma.

BIG DADDY

And what about you,
Big Daddy?
Forgetting wife,
And life,
And family, chasing dreams, making schemes
To out do
Slew
Foot.
Your master plan is to beat the odds
Play the game, make a name
For yourself.
After all, you grown ain't you?
Old Slew Foot can't possibly get one up
On you.
What you got to do
is to make enough to buy yo' way out
Of that six foot deep dirt lined condo
Waitin' for you down the way.
Say...
The possibility of power; faith Shields.
Spirit Swords, seems
Ridiculous. Doesn't it?
Like seeking HIM while HE'S findable?
Unrighteous acts can be bindable, you know?
Anyway, who is HE? You can't see HIM, or touch
HIM.

Although some nuts say they can actually feel HIM.
Cain't rightly claim to know HIM, huh?
Lord of rejection, jealousy, murder…
Satisfy, gratify, the master of the flesh.
LOVE, family, joy, peace, must all be sacrificed on
Slew Foot's alter.
Witch's Brew, Occultist whispers
Drown out the sound of
Angel's wings.
Demonic voices, offer choices.
Porn and lust, and angel dust.
The mark of the beast appears
on the souls
Of our nearest and dearest…
Friends?
Be for real. There Is a way out,
You know.
HIS word is food.
HIS word is drink.
HIS word is power.
The price? Your Pride,
Laid aside. Cleansed by the
Blood of the Lamb.
Who Is HE?
Old Slew Fool Knows.
What you gone do? Big Daddy.

On The Way To Becoming Who I Am

Just the other day, I caught myself judging others

Oh, brother

I can't begin to tell you the pitfalls of such folly

Oh golly!

There was the young lady with the weave of purple hair

How can she dare?

I wondered, with my skirt split up my thigh,

Oh, my. I had an excuse of course, the thread just popped, you know.

Surely that wasn't the same as the young huzzy in the hall.

What gall!

Just then, a still small voice

Reminded me of my purple rain spree years ago

Pregnant was I no less

Purple hair and purple dress

What was I thinking, God bless?

Suddenly the purple girl was revealed as who she is

From the reality of who I once was!

All fire and passion and potential to become

A wonderful woman of God.

Oh beware of the snare of judging others

There are usually little green monsters lurking

Behind the self righteous indignation that

Creeps into our awareness as we wonder

And reflect upon the sins of those other

Fellow human beings that cross our paths

In the ever increasing years of our earth journey.

As I continue along the road of becoming

Who I am, and what I'll be

I can't help wondering if others

See my Lord Jesus Christ in me?

Lord help me not to judge, and keep me free from sin

And wrap your children in your love

And life that never ends.

Amen

9. A Prayer to End Abortion

Earlier, we looked at the love of God. Faith works by love. We communicate with God, who is love, through prayer. God answers the prayers of His people. Please pray this prayer with us today:

Prayer to End Abortion

Lord God, I thank you today for the gift of my life,
And for the lives of all my brothers and sisters.

I know there is nothing that destroys more life than abortion,
Yet I rejoice that you have conquered death
by the Resurrection of Your Son.

I am ready to do my part in ending abortion.
Today I commit myself
Never to be silent,
Never to be passive,
Never to be forgetful of the unborn.

I commit myself to be active in the pro-life movement,
And never to stop defending life
Until all my brothers and sisters are protected,
And our nation once again becomes
A nation with liberty and justice
Not just for some, but for all.

Through Christ our Lord. Amen!

Prayer of Father Frank Pavone

Notes

Notes

Notes

Made in the USA
Lexington, KY
25 January 2011